# CRUNCHY M

## COLORING BOOK

*illustrated by*
Rachel Jones

coconut oil

RAW
MILK

Co-sleeping

eat
local

Just put a little
Breastmilk
on it

Whole Fat
Yogurt

Cloth
Diaper

Amber
Necklace

APPLE
CIDER
VINEGAR

Organic

Herbal Teas

free range
chickens

LEARN
GUT

There's an
oil
for that

SAHM

Wear
That
Baby

Detox

Chicken Pox
Be
Party

Doula

Homemade
Deodorant

Placenta

Raw
Foodie

Water
Birth

Essential
Oils

HEALTHY
EATS

Grass-Fed Beef

Fermented Foods